Japandi Living

Japanese tradition.
Scandinavian design.

Laila Rietbergen

Lannoo

Table of Contents

CHAPTER 1.
JAPANDI

Introduction	**8**
The minimalist home	**10**
The key characteristics of Japanese and Scandinavian interior design	**20**
Japandi design icons	**32**

CHAPTER 2.
LET'S JAPANDI

The principles of tidying	**40**
Lighting	**48**
Colours and shapes	**68**
Materials and textures	**92**
The art of decoration	**108**

CHAPTER 3.
LET'S GET INSPIRED

Living room	**130**
Kitchen	**152**
Bedroom	**188**
Bathroom	**210**
Workspace	**228**

CHAPTER 1.
JAPANDI

Scandinavian and Japanese design styles both encapsulate the philosophy of 'less is more', each in its own way. They celebrate refined quality, subtlety and craftsmanship and add a whole new definition to luxury. When put together, a unique concept arises, called Japandi. The word 'Japandi' is a union between the words 'Japan' and 'Scandinavia'. Japandi focuses on simplicity and on creating a peaceful and warm environment with a minimalist layout. You might even say that it's more like a frame of mind than a way of decorating a space.

To understand how these separate parts of the world collided, we have to go back to the mid-1850s, when the Japanese opened their borders after a 200-year closed-border policy. Danish naval lieutenant William Carstensen visited Japan in 1863 and became fascinated by the country, its culture and, above all, its many enticing shops. He wrote a book entitled *Japan's Capital and the Japanese* that kicked off an interest in Denmark that never quite died out. Danish designers travelled to this new, intriguing world and discovered that the Japanese concept 'wabi-sabi' celebrated the same principles as the Danish concept 'hygge': an appreciation of minimalism, natural materials and simplicity. From that time, Nordic designs started to become influenced by the oriental aesthetic. That resulted in a perfect marriage between simplicity and elegance.

The minimalist home

A simple home environment that encourages a life well lived is increasingly important under the pressures of modern life. Your home should be a welcoming, warm retreat, a place to escape and unwind that inspires and energizes. In short, it needs to be a sanctuary.

One of the key ideas behind Japandi design, and one of the strongest links between Japanese and Scandinavian philosophy, is minimalism. Japanese and Scandinavian aesthetics both aim for simplicity, and strip away – as French writer and aviator Antoine de Saint-Exupéry so appropriately put it – everything until there's nothing left but perfection. This most certainly does not mean that dwelling in a minimalist interior involves living in a spartan room without any creature comforts and having to get rid of all of your personal objects. Minimalism simply strips away ornamental layers that otherwise would be placed on top of an existing interior. Japandi's focus is on simple lines and light spaces, devoid of clutter. Japandi is a guiding principle for establishing harmony with one's environment – to create a home that is filled with quality items, one which enhances an unencumbered lifestyle devoid of excess consumerism. It invites, in short, peace into your home.

Japanese and Scandinavian minimalistic aesthetics lean heavily on the traditional principles of wabi-sabi and hygge. They may look quite different at first glance, but upon closer inspection they have a lot of similarities. Both cultures have developed in harsh natural environments and – although significantly different – at their core they are closely connected, both highly valuing nature, simplicity, authenticity and craftmanship. As well as that, both concepts accept that time goes by and that one should move along with the changing of the tide instead of working against it. 'Wabi-sabi' and 'hygge' are words that don't have a direct English translation. They are concepts or states of mind more than anything else.

Perfection is achieved, not when there is nothing more to add, but when there is nothing left to take away.
— Antoine de Saint-Exupéry (1900–1944)

Wabi-sabi

Wabi-sabi is a complex concept that derives from the principles of Zen Buddhism. It originated in China but evolved seven hundred years ago into a Japanese ideal. It was honoured by the Japanese nobility as a reaction against heavy ornamentation and lavishness. Wabi-sabi was the first step to satori or enlightenment. In modern times, wabi-sabi involves a slightly different ethos. It embraces the beauty of imperfection and being at peace with the imperfections of the world. 'Wabi' translates freely as 'rustic simplicity' or 'understated elegance'. 'Sabi' is understood as taking pleasure in the imperfect. Together, these concepts create a philosophy for life: to accept what is, to stay in the present moment and appreciate that nothing lasts for ever and nothing is perfect.

The art of imperfection: kintsugi

The Japanese practice that perhaps most exemplifies the spirit of wabi-sabi is kintsugi. Back when resources weren't so abundant, people were more likely to repair household items than replace them. Those repairs gave each object a unique appearance, their patina a silent witness to a life fully lived. Some historical sources suggest that the art of kintsugi – the practice of sealing cracks in damaged pottery with gold and lacquer – was introduced as an aesthetically pleasing solution to mending valuable ceramics. Kintsugi transforms broken pieces into a new object; the mended cracks become part of its patina and thus enhance its beauty.

Hygge

The Danish adopted the word 'hyggja' in the 18th century from Old Norwegian, in which it meant something like 'to think'. Hygge was traditionally attributed to the Scandinavian response to finding warmth and shelter after a long day working in the freezing cold. Although 'hygge' is often used to describe the way Danes survive winter, moments of hygge happen throughout the year.

Hygge is a kind of art form, developed by creating intimacy and warmth in virtually any moment. It can be celebrated alone or in groups. It's about finding happiness in simple moments. The biggest difference between hygge and wabi-sabi is hygge's emphasis on cosiness. The ways to hygge are plentiful and all promote your wellbeing, joy and comfort. To hygge is to relieve stress.

Tea ceremony

In both Scandinavian and Japanese cultures, tea and coffee are much more than just delicious hot drinks. Drinking them is an expression of an attitude towards life and an opportunity to relax in everyday life. These drinking ceremonies bring people together and have grown into important every day traditions.

The Japanese tea ceremony, or chanoyu ('hot water for tea'), is an elaborate ritual of serving green tea ('matcha'), along with some sweets. There are four philosophies portrayed in a Japanese tea ceremony: harmony, respect, purity and tranquility. The ceremony is a way to relieve the stress of everyday life, even for just a short while, by immersing in the Zen aesthetics of serenity and peace. These two qualities give the tea ceremony its simple and quiet appearance.

Fika

Fika originated in Sweden and is an important part of Swedish culture. It's much more than your regular coffee break and that's because the intend behind it is mighty different. Fika is about genuinely slowing down. It's a break from activity, to step back and to enjoy a cup of coffee or tea and something to eat with friends, family or colleagues. Fika can therefore be therapeutic, promotes wellbeing and productivity. Some companies even add a clause to contracts stating that employees are entitled to fika breaks.

The key characteristics of Japanese and Scandinavian interior design

When you think about minimalistic living, you are most likely to think of Scandinavian or Japanese interior design. Where they differ, they complement each other. Where Japanese interiors are sleek, Scandinavian ones are rustic. The rich, earthen colours of Japanese design help to keep the monochrome palette of Scandinavian homes from feeling austere. You might say it was only a matter of time before they mixed into the new aesthetic known as Japandi. Now let's zoom in on the particular characteristics of Japanese and Scandinavian interior design.

Traditional Japanese interior design

Simplicity and purity have been adopted in Japanese architecture all through time. Japanese architecture and interior design give preference to craftsmanship. Overall, homes have ample, open and highly adaptable spaces with a lot of natural light. Also greenery is used as much as possible in design ideas. This is a way of bringing the natural world into the home. Furnishings and decorations are kept to a minimum. Walls have soft, earthen colours, paper screens and bamboo or wooden finishes. Lighting is usually gentle, provided by paper-covered lamps or ceramic lanterns. The overall effect is soothing, peaceful and calm.

Traditional Japanese-style rooms come in two basic types: shoin and sukiya.

Shoin-style rooms originally served as studies for the wealthy, before gradually becoming more commonplace as reception and living spaces. Typically they have a built-in desk (tsukeshoin) incorporated below a window, an alcove and built-in shelves called chigaidana. Shoin-style rooms became popular in residences in the Muromachi period (1336–1573). Additional characteristics that developed in shoin rooms include floors covered entirely with tatami mats, fusuma sliding doors and shoji doors.

The second style, sukiya, is a variation on shoin that has subtle artistic differences. Sukiya-style architecture was originally used for teahouses. Based on an aesthetic of naturalness and rustic simplicity, buildings in this style are intended to harmonize with their surroundings. Timber construction is employed, with wood left in a natural state – sometimes with the bark still attached. Walls are typically made of clay. Great attention is paid to detail and proportion, and the effect is one of refined simplicity.

Main components of the Japanese interior

Tatami mat floor
In a traditional Japanese home, people sit on traditional flooring material in the form of tatami mats. Made from woven rush straw, tatami has a soft and gentle springiness that makes it a comfortable base for cushions (such as the traditional Japanese cushions called zabuton) and as supportive as a mattress. Indeed, for Japanese people tatami is so strongly associated with the comforts of home that it is not uncommon for people to say such things as 'I would be happy to die on tatami.' Tatami mats were found in virtually all Japanese homes until modern, wooden and carpeted floors started to replace them in recent decades.

Zaisu
The use of tatami flooring has determined the kind of furniture Japanese people use. The zaisu, for instance, is a Japanese chair with no legs and a normal chair back.

Chabudai and kotatsu
Chabudai are low short-legged tables used for having tea or dining. Kotatsu, which are often used during winter, are covered by a blanket and heated underneath.

Fusuma
Another important aspect of traditional Japanese interiors is adaptability. By using sliding doors called fusuma, a large room can be converted into separate rooms. Historically, fusuma have been canvases for famous painters and some elaborately painted examples may be seen in temples and palaces.

Shōji is another type of sliding door, made of translucent paper on a wooden frame. They give a degree of privacy but also allow soft natural light to flow into the room. Yukimi shōji have a sliding panel at their base, behind which is a sheet of glass. Yukimi literally means 'snow viewing'; this type of screen allows you to stay warm inside while viewing the winter scene outside. Portable room dividers are tsuitate partitioning screens and byōbu folding screens.

Ranma
Long before the invention of air conditioning, Japanese homes were designed to maximize air circulation, which is particularly important during the hot summer months. Ranma are wooden transoms that are typically found above fusuma in traditional Japanese-style rooms. Ranma are often beautifully carved and add an ornate touch to the overall simple Japanese interior.

Materials
In Japan, aesthetics are based on a relationship with nature. Japanese design therefore focuses on natural materials like bamboo, woven straw, rattan, paper, ceramics and (predominantly) wood. The use of these materials is not just limited to furniture; it may be used on walls, floors and ceilings. The Japanese aesthetic also encourages to bring in plants inside spaces.

Right page: A tatami-floored room is still not uncommon, and the size of a room is therefore sometimes measured by how many mats fit inside it. Tatamis are made in standard sizes, twice as long as wide, about 0.88 m x 1.76 m depending on the region.

Left page: The major elements of a traditional Japanese interior captured in one image: a tatami-mat floor, a chabudai table and zaisu chairs adorned with zabuton.
Above left: Adaptability is an important aspect of the traditional Japanese interior. Sliding doors give the opportunity to make a room more intimate by closing them, or to ventilate it by opening them.
Above right: Zaisu, chairs without legs.

Traditional Scandinavian style

Scandinavian interiors are a balance between functionality and aesthetics, inspired by a blend of styles from Denmark, Sweden and Norway. While Finland and Iceland are often included in this definition, they're officially not part of Scandinavia. The Scandinavian design movement in its current form emerged in the early 20th century when designers such as Arne Jacobsen, Verner Panton (Denmark), Josef Frank (Sweden) and Alvar Aalto (Finland) began producing their work, kicking off the so-called golden age of Scandinavian design. Contemporary designers continue that legacy today with award-winning designs that look as elegantly simple and visionary as the creations that preceded them.

Scandinavian design is characterized by a minimal, clean approach that seeks to combine functionality with beauty. Scandinavian design is far from fussy or profuse; it simply shows the essence of a product. Furnishings and decorations are kept to a minimum, and this lack of clutter makes the style aesthetically pleasing. Each space has a calm and feel-good quality that permeates the atmosphere. Lighting is a huge part of Scandinavian design as the Nordic countries get so little of it naturally during the winter. The style is also based on people's close relationship with nature. Natural materials such as cotton, wool, linen and wood are commonly used, as are house plants.

The Scandinavian palette is neutral and monochromatic. Wood is light to complement these neutrals. Traditional pattern designs are typically simple, botanical illustrations in a repetitive or symmetrical style that contrasts with a light-coloured backdrop. Furthermore, pops of colour are added as accents. Those give a room a sense of balance while avoiding the dullness of a plain neutral room.

Left page: Cold winters ask for warm accessories with loads of texture.
Right page: A typical Scandinavian palette: a neutral base of wood and shades of grey. Flowers and accessories add pops of colour.

Left page: Like the Japanese, the Scandinavians often finish their walls with wood. They add contrast with accents of bright colours such as red and ice blue.
Right page: House plants reflect the Scandinavians' close relationship with nature. They bring the natural world into your home.

Japandi design icons

These design icons present a perfect marriage between elegance and minimalism and are therefore textbook examples of the Japandi aesthetic.

Wishbone chair, Carl Hansen
To this day, the hundred steps required to make a Wishbone chair are mostly done by hand, creating an elegant and – although more than seventy years old – truly timeless work of simplicity. In its graceful shape the maker Hans J. Wegner hints at modernist ideals and Japanese design.

Butterfly stool, Sory Yanagi

Japanese craftmanship and Western technique come together in this stool, created in 1954 by Sori Yanagi. It is composed of two curved pieces of plywood (a technique developed by American power couple Charles and Ray Eames) which together form the shape of a butterfly.

Akari light sculptures, Isamu Noguchi

Right page: Since 1951, Akari light sculptures have been made using the same methods as those used for Japanese Gifu lanterns. By combining sculpted shapes and light cast through handmade paper on a bamboo frame, Isamu Noguchi brought traditional Japanese materials to the modern home. Nowadays, you will see lots of lights that are definitely inspired by his design, like this one.

Hashira lamp, Norm Architects for MENU space
A fusion of tradition and modernity, this lantern-like design is a reference to traditional Japanese rice-paper lamps.

CHAPTER 2.
LET'S JAPANDI

How wonderful it would be if, immediately upon entering your home, you were greeted with a style that was natural, muted and inviting! Japandi is both casual and elegant, comfortable and decluttered. It is marked by muted and earthy colours such as browns and beiges that make a space feel warm and embracing. Japandi doesn't use designs that compete against each other for attention. Investing in a small number of high-quality furniture and lighting pieces is the preferred way to achieve the Japandi aesthetic. Always remember that less is more when it comes to Japandi. It may be tempting to purchase cheap fast-fashion items, but it is better to purchase pieces you know you'll love for years to come. On the following pages, I'll take you through the most important aspects of a Japandi interior and how to incorporate them into your home and heart.

The principles of tidying

One of the major attractions of Japandi is its tidiness. This means more than just tidying once in a while by putting items away in cupboards. It also means more than getting rid of things. The Japandi philosophy of decluttering is about creating surroundings that support mindfulness and peace – about living with less and buying with more conscience. Also, think about how fast you would be able to clean a home that's not filled to the brim with stuff!

The thought of decluttering an entire home may feel overwhelming. In this chapter, I'll take you through the main principles of tidying and decluttering your home. Some may work for you, some won't, but these principles will help you make your first steps towards the streamlined, organized home that is at the heart of the Japandi aesthetic.

The Marie Kondo principle of tidying

The KonMarie method™ of tidying your house is world renowned and has a lot of similarities to the Japandi approach to a tidy home. Marie Kondo believes that tidying is a celebration, a special send-off for things that will be departing from the house. By asking people if something sparks joy (and advising that if it doesn't, to let it go) she helps them to bring order to their homes and, ultimately, to their lives and mental health. The Marie Kondo principle of tidying and decluttering is about owning less and being in control of one's environment and life.

The Japandi way of decluttering and organizing

Since Japandi focuses on clean lines and open spaces, reducing clutter is key to achieving the Japandi style. The best way to make decluttering easier is to do it in stages.

There are two ways of tidying a home: by room and by category. Marie Kondo believes that you should tidy by category and not room by room. I think there are pros and cons to each. Let's look at them in turn to help you decide which would work better for you. It's like choosing an exercise: if you do what works best for you, it is more likely that you will commit to it in a more sustainable fashion.

Tidying room by room

The advantage of tidying room by room is that you will touch and assess every object in your home. That gives you the opportunity to discover all the objects that belong to one category as you go. Objects (books, for example) are often spread throughout the house. By sorting room by room, you go through every cupboard, drawer, nook and cranny and come to know where all the objects in a category are. Once you know where everything is, you can sort them and give them a fitting space.

Don't plan to tackle your entire house in one day. Focus on one room, one space, or even one zone within a room (such as your office desk or that drawer full of random items), completing the job fully before moving on to the next space. And remember, decluttering is not about discarding stuff at random. Consider Marie Kondo's words while tidying: does it spark joy, or is it time to let it go?

Tidying by category

Marie Kondo encourages individuals to tidy in categories – first clothes, then books, paperwork, miscellaneous items and, last, sentimental items. In other words, you tidy things in the same category in one go. For example, when tidying your clothes the first step is to gather every item of clothing from the entire house in one spot. This allows you to see exactly how much you have. Go through the pile and decide – to use Kondo's words – what sparks joy and what can go to the donation pile.

Tidying (or sorting) by category works particularly well for those who are already pretty well organized and already have a space for everything in their house. It gives a good insight into what your collection of socks/books/tableware and so on contains. Tidying by category also works well if you want to achieve something in a short time. Tidying one sock drawer feels less overwhelming than tidying a whole space at once.

The four-box method

To help you declutter, take four baskets, bins or boxes designated as follows: 'trash', 'give away', 'keep' and 'store'. Bring these boxes into each room as you declutter. It's necessary to evaluate each item individually, so take the time to focus on its purpose in your life before you sort it. Trying to sort too fast or process too many items at once will result in very full 'keep' and 'store' boxes.

Decide on permanent storage spaces for commonly used items such as chargers, keys, toys and remote controls. You could establish a 'put away' box for items that tend to wander round the house (like that coffee cup that's still on your office desk). Collect them in this box during your moments of downtime throughout the day and put things back in their proper places later.

The 80/20 rule

By storing 80 per cent of your possessions and putting 20 per cent on display, you can further reduce visual 'noise'. Consider this as a guideline, by the way, not a rule. It may help you to attain those clean Japandi lines you're aiming for!

First, decide for each room which items you'd like to keep in view. What remains may be put into storage. The 80/20 rule gives you the opportunity to decide on the right amount of storage for each – what you need to put 80 per cent out of sight and where you want a space to display the things that spark joy.

365 items in 365 days

In addition to achieving good karma, you could give away 365 items from your home in 365 days. If you find this challenging, you could give away one item a week for 52 weeks instead. Give them to charity, to people who really need a certain object, or just to gain the satisfaction of giving away something you have carefully selected.

Lighting

From the 17th century, traditional oil lamps (andon) devised from handmade paper, bamboo, wood or metal were generally used in Japan. The andon created the minimum level of light required to function in the darkness of night, while not altering the ambience. These traditional lights were highly ingenious and well designed. In Scandinavia, the light of the hearth remained the most usual source of lighting until the adoption of candles in the 19th century. The return of natural light is still greatly celebrated, with at its height the celebration of midsummer (the lightest day of the year and the start of summer). In general, natural (day)light is of great importance to Japanese and Scandinavian interior design.

However, our homes are generally not at their brightest when we are at home. We therefore have to turn to clever lighting that adds to the aesthetic we're aiming for. Japandi lighting sets mood and tone and can instantly make a room feel comfortable and cosy.

Frederik Alexander Werner (Designer & Partner at Norm Architects): 'In Scandinavia where the winter months are long and dark and much of our time is spent inside, the way we illuminate our homes is very important. Personally, I treasure the use of filtered omni light – which is why washi paper lamps work so well. By using the right light source, you do not only create a warm and welcoming atmosphere, but you also get the benefit of the structures and tactility in the paper itself.'

Light and Japandi

The purpose of light in Japandi is to add ambience to a room and create a relaxing atmosphere. Overall, Japandi lighting is functional, beautiful and sculptural without being overwhelming. Subtleness is key. Japandi features warm, diffuse light that feels close to candlelight or the light of a lantern. Stronger lighting is reserved for rooms where it is needed, such as the kitchen and bathroom.

Artificial light affects our moods just as much as natural daylight. Proper lighting should be practical and aesthetically attractive, whether you're striving to create a Japandi style or anything else. There is, in short, far more to good lighting than simply choosing an attractive lampshade. Good artificial light consists of three fundamental elements, with which you can achieve the perfect balance between style and comfort: decorative lighting, task lighting and accent lighting. A successful lighting scheme will always have a mix of these three.

Decorative lighting

Ambient lighting provides the foundation and general illumination for a room. Apart from the basic lighting functionality it provides, ambient lighting enhances the sense of warmth and depth of a space.

Left page: This modern interpretation of antique portable oil lamps spreads beautiful soft light, thanks to the translucent opal glass.
Right page: Decorative lights complement and enhance their surroundings. The oak cylindrical lamp base produces a warm, modern atmosphere while the subtle patterned shade diffuses the light into a soft glow.

Task lighting

Task lighting has entirely practical uses, providing you with the illumination you need for specific activities around your home. It is designed to create a shadow-free environment for the times when you are involved in such daily things as reading a book, cooking and working.

Accent lighting

Accent lighting is intended to highlight a specific object or area. It is typically brighter than decorative lighting. It will create depth in a room if properly applied.

Scandinavian classics

Left page: Lighting design pioneer Poul Henningsen (1894–1967) devised the PH 5 pendant in 1958. Not only does it serve as a beautiful sculptural element whether it is turned on or off, it also encompasses the duality of design and light. The PH 5's majority of light shines downward into the space it illuminates rather than into people's eyes, thanks to Henningsen's ingenious five-shade system. The pendant holds a light bulb, producing the ideal combination of downward and lateral light, while also gently illuminating the fixture itself. Interior anti-glare rings and reflectors ensure a warm glow of light that complements the daily rhythm of natural light. Decades later, the PH 5 remains a best-selling design.

Right page: In 1971, Verner Panton (1926–1998) designed a lamp that would become an icon. Panton was famous for his innovative designs and his pioneering use of materials, colours and shapes, which made him one of the most influential designers and architects of his time. With Panthella, Panton wanted to create a graphic and figurative lamp that could stand alone in a room, like a sculpture. The domed Panthella is designed to shape light and gently illuminate the surroundings to create an ideal ambience.

Use the interplay of sunlight and shadow to full advantage for an optimum serene effect.

Colours and shapes

One of the major differences between the Japanese and Scandinavian styles is their colour palettes. Scandinavian interiors feature clean whites and off-whites with pops of green, blue or even pastels; whereas Japanese interiors are often a reflection of nature, darker in comparison, featuring moody browns, deep greens and taupes, yet warm and tranquil.

The Japandi palette is a symphony between these two palettes. It combines the light colour scheme of Scandinavia with the darker and earthy tones from Japan. The neutrals provide a cosy canvas, while their darker counterparts offer up a balanced contrast. And contrast is everything in an overall monochrome palette.

Note that the Japandi colour palette is calming and rooted in warm neutrals, so be careful not to use too much clean white. Warm whites look as clean as stark whites without being sterile. I'll explain more about shades of warm white on page 72.

Colours

A monochrome palette creates harmony, but harmony alone won't make a space look interesting. In fact, too much of the same creates monotony and boredom. It's important to add visual interest to a space by using contrast. But how do you add contrast to a space?

When you place two elements with opposing characteristics together you create contrast. You can add contrast by pairing soft and dark hues, or by adding interesting shapes, textures or materials. You'll read more about typical Japandi textures on page 93, but let us dive a bit deeper into adding contrast using colour and paint finishes first.

Choosing your Japandi colour palette is the most important aspect of adding the aesthetic to your home, yet it may be the most intimidating part. Nothing is as personal as colour. There are a few tips and tricks to help you pick your personal perfect Japandi palette.

When choosing a palette, start with three colours. Three is a number that won't immediately overwhelm you. Of course, you don't have to limit yourself to these, but doing so may make things a bit easier. There's nothing wrong with using photographs from books or the internet as inspiration, but there are a few things to keep in mind to avoid disappointment. Images from such sources as these may not reproduce well. Also the lighting you have may be entirely different from what is in the photograph. What looks perfect in the original may not work in your home.

Your home already has a distinctive style. It may look very different from that photograph you love, but you know a lot about it. You know where the light comes in, which rooms are bright and which are maybe a bit gloomy. You'll be aware your furniture has a theme, too. Understanding your own style and theme will help you get an overall idea of the colours you want to apply to your decor. You could also look into your wardrobe. Is there a favourite item of clothing of a particular colour that you're drawn to? That may be your starting point – your colour inspiration.

Before committing to a palette, consider two more elements: lighting and sight lines – how the hues look when you see them from other rooms. Rather than choosing paint by looking at small swatches, buy sample-size cans of colours that appeal and paint them on big pieces of paper. Place these paint samples on the wall, apart from each other but close enough to see both how the colours work alone and with each other. Remember that lighting (natural and artificial) will change the way specific colours look and feel. Choose whatever feels right to you; there is no right or wrong.

> Don't be afraid to add darker accents such as charcoal and earthy tones to your Japandi interior. They will add contrast without exaggerating or breaking the minimalist harmony of the look.

How to pick the perfect shade of white

White is white, right? Alas, it is not. Finding the right shade of white can be surprisingly challenging. The reason some whites end up looking yellow, pink or even purple is that most white paints are not pure white. They are a very light shade of a colour. That colour is the undertone and it will show up ever so slightly once you paint your walls. These tips will help you choose the right white for your Japandi space.

There's an easy trick to help you avoid choosing a white that's too creamy or too icy. All you have to do is hold your paint swatch up to a plain piece of printer paper. This will help you determine whether the white swatch you have is a warm white (with a red, yellow or orange undertone) or a cool white (with a blue or grey tone). A cool white works best together with cool tones such as blue or green. Warmer whites work better with warm colours such as terracotta. As pointed out earlier, warm whites may feel as clean as stark white without looking sterile, and they match the warm, embracing Japandi aesthetic better. Even hues such as the palest taupe or griege may lend that clean, fresh but warm feeling to a space.

The 60-30-10 principle of choosing colour

There's an easy way to come up with a balanced colour palette for your space. It is called the 60-30-10 principle of choosing colour. It states that 60 per cent of the room (floor, walls, big pieces of furniture) should be in a dominant colour, 30 per cent (curtains, rugs, smaller pieces of furniture) in a secondary colour or texture, and the last 10 per cent (art, decorations, floor cushions, etc.) should be in an accent colour.

The overall colour of the room represents 60 per cent. This will be the background colour with which you will complement the remaining 30 and 10 per cent.

The next number in the principle is 30 per cent. That will be the secondary colour in your space. It will support the main colour, but be different enough to give the room interest. Think of it this way: you'll be using half as much of this colour as you did of your main colour.

The last 10 per cent is your accent colour. It may be bolder – in Japandi's case charcoal or a dark earthy green or brown, or a subtle pastel – and depends on the look you want. The 10 per cent is what gives the room character or keeps it more neutral; it's up to you. Remember that contrast gives a space interest. The 10 per cent proportion may be vital in establishing this.

Choosing colours should not be a gamble. It should be a conscious decision. Colours have a meaning and a function.
— Verner Panton (1926–1998)

Paint finishes

A different kind of paint finish may add subtle contrast to a space. There are six different types, varying by sheen and durability. For walls it's best to go with as little sheen as possible. Flat paint will absorb the most light and give you the truest colour. It also helps to hide imperfections on walls, though on the other hand it shows wear and smudges more than the other types. It's therefore advisable to go with an eggshell or satin sheen in high-traffic areas. Also note: the darker the colour, the glossier it will seem.

Gloss
A gloss paint finish is shiny with a glass-like surface. Gloss finishes aren't often used in the Japandi aesthetic, but they are seen on high-use surfaces such as door frames.

Semi-gloss
Semi-gloss paint finish has high durability and a sleek look. It is resistant to moisture and wear. Semi-gloss is good for rooms where moisture, drips and grease stains are a challenge, such as kitchens and bathrooms.

Satin sheen
Satin has a slightly higher sheen than eggshell, meaning that it is more reflective and more durable. It's a great choice for painting moderate to high-traffic areas or areas that have some exposure to moisture, such as kitchens and bathrooms.

Eggshell
Eggshell looks and feels somewhat flat but has a little lustre, like a chicken's egg.

Matte
Matte finish is nearly as shine free as flat/chalk, providing excellent cover with depth, and also with slightly more durability.

Flat/chalk paint
Flat paint has a finish that does not reflect light, resulting in no sheen at all. It tends to hide rough surfaces and gives a chalky appearance and velvety feel to them. This is also a disadvantage because it will tend to hold on to dirt and stains. It's much harder to clean than glossier paints.

Clay plaster

Clay plaster is a mixture of clay and sand that makes an environmentally friendly alternative to conventional paint. Clay occurs naturally in a range of colours. It can be tinted with pigments to offer an almost unlimited colour palette. It has an earthy and soft patina.

Colour systems and colour codes

Instead of having to describe a tint, nowadays we can rely on colour codes or numbers. The NCS Colour or Natural Colour System originated in Sweden and is based on what the word implies: natural colours. The colours are exactly how the eyes naturally see red, yellow, blue, green, white and black. Other hues within the NCS are the result of a merging of colours. The fusion of red and yellow produces orange, for example. The NCS colour system is commonly used in painting, decorating and designing and is used worldwide. You may know the European RAL colour system, a colour-matching system that originated in Germany. RAL consists of 213 colours and is still in use. It's used for metals, and in a lot of countries for wall and wood paints as well.

Left page: You easily change the atmosphere of a room and add contrast by painting a loose panel in a colour of your choice.
Right page: Bold colours don't necessarily make a room look stuffy or overcrowded. Combined with Japandi's minimalistic principles, they make the perfect serene atmosphere.

Shapes

Flow and form are the primary pillars of Japandi. It draws on finding beauty in the imperfect and in nature and comfort, and revolves round a contrasted, minimal approach. Japandi shapes are therefore nature inspired, with simple, clean, organic lines. Typical Japandi designs are founded on what is known as biomorphism, which bases artistic design elements on naturally occurring patterns or shapes reminiscent of nature and living organisms. Taken to an extreme, it attempts to force naturally occurring shapes onto functional devices. Well-known examples of biomorphism are Surrealism and Art Nouveau, but it's also seen in industrial design such as the work of Isamu Nochugi and Alvar Aalto.

Bring in furniture with strong, deliberate outlines and softened edges, low to the floor or on legs, to help enhance a feeling of space. More sculptural elements, such as an impressive lamp or a statement piece of art, will add further interest and contrast to the space. They have a greater effect when left solo, which is why they fit the aesthetic so well.

There are three types of sight line to consider when decorating a space: horizontal, vertical and organic. When combined, these lines establish a sense of harmony, contrast and unity. In other words, they bring structure, creativity and a sense of direction to a space and help your eyes travel through it in a pleasurable manner. Horizontal lines are often found in tables, chairs and similar furnishings. Vertical lines typically come from doors, windows and tall structures such as bookcases. A space may seem too heavy if the design includes only horizontal and vertical lines. Japandi's curved lines add a soft feel to the whole. By adding curves through patterns and textures (rugs and fabrics) or structures (furniture and accessories), you combine the three types of lines and bring balance to the space.

Right page: The Zen rug is inspired by Japanese gardens and mimics the ripples of water.

Materials and textures

Contrast is essential when it comes to a good interior design. It keeps things balanced and provides visual interest. With the right mixture of materials (and therefore texture) you make sure the important elements of a space stand out. Texture is particularly important if you're working with the Japandi colour palette, where the shades are very similar.

Texture typically pertains to the surface quality of any material. Considering materials therefore means considering texture. There are two types: visual and actual. Visual textures relate to appearance only, as in marble; actual textures are both seen and felt, as in wool. When opposing textures are combined, they enhance each other. The outcome is the creation of balance and contrast.

Organic and natural materials take pride of place in Scandinavian and Japanese design, reflecting their important relationship with nature. Japandi focuses entirely on natural materials and textures. As the quality of natural materials tends to be high, that translates into increased longevity. Even when natural materials start to show signs of wear, they tend to look better than their artificial counterparts. The worn look usually translates into an attractive patina that makes the material look more attractive instead of ragged. Read more about wabi-sabi and patina on pages 12 and 14.

Apart from bringing nature inside and being good for the environment, materials such as wood, bamboo, wool, paper, leather and rattan also add a warm and cosy feel to your Japandi interior. So, let's examine the most important Japandi materials and textures and how to integrate them into your space.

All that you require to start a home are a room, a tatami and Akari.
— Isamu Noguchi (1904–1988)

Wood

One of Japandi's staples is wood, which can be used for everything from floors and furniture to tableware. It's a very practical material, hard wearing and easy to maintain. When it comes to wood, if you are aiming to bring a more Scandinavian feel to your home, choose light, untreated wood tones. If you are drawn more to the Japanese style, look for dark shades of wood furniture. The grain of wood adds an interesting texture to the home environment, constituting natural decoration. Look out for beautiful wooden coffee tables with knots in the wood. A subtle way of introducing wooden detailing is to hang posters in wooden frames. Another great way to add texture to a Japandi interior is with a slatted accent wall. Slatted walls create visual and architectural interest within a space.

Natural stone

Natural stone is not only durable; it also celebrates imperfection and brings texture to a space. In the Japandi aesthetic, it is often used in bathrooms and kitchens (see pages 210 and 153), and for coffee tables, side tables and dining tables in several shapes. Natural stones which are most often used in this style are various kinds of limestone, terrazzo and marble.

Bamboo

Sustainability is at the core of Japandi. Bamboo is a fast-growing material, and its use helps to decrease deforestation. It is therefore a popular sustainable material option. Bamboo is extremely durable, and its neutral colour means it can be incorporated perfectly into the Japandi aesthetic. It's used for flooring, kitchen cabinets, accessories and even wall coverings.

Paper

Thirteen hundred years ago, the Japanese developed a paper called washi which is made using traditional Japanese methods and which is stronger and more durable than its industrially produced counterpart. Traditionally, this paper was not only used for writing and painting, but also for lanterns, umbrellas, clothing and shoji sliding doors and walls. Washi is still much used in traditional art forms, book binding and origami.

Home furnishings made from paper – such as lights, minimalist wallpapers and origami-inspired wall decorations – are items suitable for use in order to introduce Japandi's serenity and simplicity into your home.

Fabrics

Because Japandi embraces nature, it calls for the selection of eco-friendly fabrics for clothing and for furnishings in your home. Make sure you opt for textured natural fabrics such as cotton, linen and wool for upholstery, curtains, drapery, cushions and pillows; then you will not be in conflict with Japandi's basic design principles.

Changing accessories such as floor cushions and rugs is a simple way to update your home according to the seasons. Use linen-covered items during summer, for example, and replace them with woollen covers during winter.

Flooring

Flooring is a crucial part of any interior and can easily make or break a space. It is a large surface that can have a powerful impact on visual perspective, look and feel.

Japandi floors are usually made of hardwood. Wood floors are comfortable and durable, and nothing quite compares to the character and warmth they bring to every room in the house that has them. Once you've decided on a wood floor, you need to consider the finish for your new surface. Hardwood floors need a finish for proper protection, and choosing the right one depends on the look and performance you want. There are many different types of hardwood flooring, each with distinct advantages and disadvantages. Which one is right for your floor(s) will depend on the durability, moisture protection and glossy sheen you want for your space.

Polished concrete or cast flooring also fits the aesthetic, but do keep in mind that those options produce a slightly less warm feel than a wooden floor.

Creating a moodboard

Interior designers often use materials and textures to make a moodboard for a space. Making a moodboard helps you hone your visual ideas as you decide on the right kind of floor and wall finish and the overall atmosphere you're aiming for.

There are three types of interior design moodboard. The first type brings furniture and decor pieces together to help you see how all the pieces will fit and go together stylistically. You can create a moodboard with a collection of textures, paint colours, furnishings, rugs, artworks and so on. You can be as detailed as you want, or as simple as you want. This gives you an overall vibe regarding your interior design and will provide you with a helpful reference point throughout the design process. The last type of moodboard is much more abstract. It's a collection of inspirational images that together evoke a feeling or emotion that sets a vibe or mood for a space.

Whatever means you use to create your moodboard – whether by using materials and textures, digitally or with magazine clippings – be aware that it's a great tool for pulling your design ideas into one place and seeing how they work together.

The art of decoration

By combining Scandinavian homely comforts with Japanese imperfection, you get an aesthetic with a focus on practicality and comfort merging the two styles to produce a scaled-back, luxurious yet cosy feel. This creates a place that offers calm and peace, away from the hectic world outside. The philosophies behind Japanese and Scandinavian design languages call for accessories that prioritize functionality over decoration.

The most important points to keep in mind while incorporating Japandi into your design style are to keep things simple and embrace minimalism. It's an exercise in restraint, where space, lighting and objects play equally important roles. A Japandi home radiates natural beauty created by a set of carefully selected objects that deliver maximum impact. Nothing has to be perfect, but everything should have a place and purpose. Japandi decoration is focused on craftsmanship; things aren't made to be thrown away. It's important to look for pieces that will stand the test of time and work with your decor for years to come. And if you do eventually want to part with one, you should still be able to donate it to a friend or a charity, so that it finds a new home. It is, in short, an antidote to the one-time-use culture we have embraced for so long.

Art

Art is an indispensable addition to an interior. It gives a space a personal touch, and a good piece of art can really tie a room together. Choosing art is personal and there is no accounting for individual taste, but there are a few tips and tricks to help you choose artworks that really fit the Japandi aesthetic.

Japandi is dominated by natural materials and a tranquil colour scheme. It won't come as a surprise that you'll find the same palette in a typical piece of Japandi art. Minimalist or monochrome art fits the aesthetic comfortably, as does art that uses contrasts such as neutrals (beige, white, grey) with dark browns, traditional Japanese reds, blacks or pops of pale pink or sky blue. Pastels pay tribute to Scandinavian art, which often features a neutral colour palette combined with bright pastels and busy patterns. This kind of visual weight adds oomph to an overall minimalistic interior.

Another way to create a statement with art is by size. In a Japandi interior you'll mostly find large pieces of art – statement pieces – on the walls. One of these makes a focal point in a room and will help to create a magnificent and impressive space. Before choosing a size, consider the amount of furniture in the room and assess your ceilings. Are they high, vaulted or voluminous, allowing for a grand picture? Or are they low, in which case a lower canvas height with landscape orientation might work better? Also consider the viewing distance. You need to be able to look at a piece of art from a certain distance to appreciate it fully. It's therefore advisable to choose small pieces of art for narrow spaces such as hallways and staircases. A good rule of thumb for measuring viewing distance is multiplying the diagonal of the picture by 1.5.

How to create a gallery wall

If you are decorating a small space or do not have a large enough budget for substantial original paintings, a gallery wall is a good solution. It is also great for showcasing small pieces of art while commanding the attention of a room.

Before you start your gallery wall, don't go buying a large number of pieces on a whim. A captivating Japandi gallery wall will look and feel coordinated. As you start collecting, think about the scale of your assemblage and the layout you envisage. Do you want to display items that are all the same size or work with a mixture of different sizes? Do you want neat rows or an organic arrangement?

For original artworks or prints, select colours that go with the tone of the room you want to display them in. Look for ways to tie disparate pieces together, through colour or framing. This adds to the calm and balanced feel of the Japandi style. You can combine traditional vintage Japanese reproductions with modern Scandi art, for example, by selecting images with the same colour scheme. Think about the feeling you want to create in the room. If you're creating an art wall for the bedroom, it's sensible to choose a calm colour palette, whereas it's fine to create a stunning entrance in your hallway, perhaps with a collection of lovely postcards that evoke good memories.

Once your collection is complete, it's time to make a template. Measure your wall space and lay your items on the floor. Alternatively, you could trace the outside of the frames onto paper, cut them out and move them round on the wall, using masking tape. Start in the middle with the largest artwork and work from there to keep the whole balanced. Generally speaking, the centre of the art wall should be about 182 cm (6 ft) from the floor. Allow a little space between the frames. Decide whether odd or even numbers work best. Sometimes even numbers work well in regimented groups of the same size but more random arrangements or collections work better with odd numbers. Stand back and look at them together. Does anything jump out as wrong? If yes, switch it or take it out. Maybe there's room to add more. Once you're satisfied with the template, take a photograph of it. Using a pencil and eraser, draw lightly on the walls where the top corners of the frames will be. Measure and mark how much lower down the picture frame you want your nail holes. Start hammering and get your gallery arrangement onto the wall.

Greenery

Nature is a central element in both Scandinavian and Japanese cultures, and a very effective way of integrating natural elements into the Japandi style is by adding plants. Japandi interiors don't tend to go overboard on interior plants, but they do prefer greens to be big and bold. This is because it's easier to achieve optical balance and calm with one or two green statement pieces than with several surfaces filled with plants. Don't fret if you're a passionate plant collector, though; this doesn't mean that you may not use greens freely in a Japandi-style home.

The right plant for the right place

Whether you want to have one statement piece in your Japandi interior, or a bunch of houseplants grouped together, you will have some preferences when it comes to choosing what to display. So how do you pick your perfect houseplant?

People often make the mistake of choosing which plant they want before they know where it is to go. The truth is, you should first decide where you want it before you decide which to buy. Different plants will thrive in different spots, depending on the amount of space and light available. Light, temperature and humidity are the main things to keep in mind when choosing a good spot for your plant. Different plants have their own individual preferences so it's worthwhile to do some research. In short: design with your plants' needs in mind!

In a minimalist, uncluttered home, plants are a great way to bring in colour and a soft, natural touch. An attractive aspect of Scandinavian interiors is that the style encompasses groups of indoor potted plants while keeping the whole look balanced and beautiful. You can introduce this calm and balanced ambience by putting your plants in the same kinds of pot, in muted or neutral colours. When you place together plants that have contrasting heights and sizes, the look becomes more organic, natural and cohesive, which adds to the optical balance you seek to find.

You can add an extra dimension to your plant display by hanging plants from a high position. Not only will you save valuable space on shelves and window sills in this way, but you can display some species to much better effect. It also keeps them away from pets or children.

Typical Japandi houseplants (big and small) are *Ficus lyrata*, *Polyscias scutellaria* (Fabian), *Ficus nitida*, *Pachira* (air purifying, both big and small species), *Ficus microcarpa* (Ginseng bonsai, big and small), *Spathiphyllum* (Peace lily, air purifying), *Polyscias fruticosa* and *Ficus benjamina*.

Did you know that grouping plants is not only for aesthetic effect? It helps them to grow better because they create their own microclimate.

Flowers and vessels

Japanese and Scandinavian designs are strongly inspired by nature, and the pottery of both cultures is distinctive and pure. Scandinavian pottery is one of the most popular forms of art, with a rich history that dates back several centuries. The earliest forms of ceramics in Japan were made about ten thousand years ago. Both Scandinavian and Japanese interiors showcase the beautiful products of hand craftsmanship, so it won't come as a surprise that an empty vase can be as much of a piece of art as the flowers you put in it.

On that note, Japandi has a minimalist take on flower arrangements, so you don't need a plethora of fresh flowers to make a style statement. A great way of creating a minimalist flower arrangement is ikebana, love to share more about ikebana with you on page 121.

An effective way of integrating natural elements in a Japandi interior is to display one or two thin branches in a vase. Get your branches to stand up in position by using clear plastic tape to create a grid on the mouth of your container before placing your stems.

> Some vases are not designed for fresh flowers. Your beautiful handmade ceramic vase may have an unglazed interior that water will permeate. This is bad for both vase and the surface beneath. When you purchase or receive a vase, be sure to find out whether it's intended to hold water. If not, use it for dried flowers only, or as a decorative object rather than a functional one.

The perfect way to get affordable, eye-catching vessels for your arrangements is to look for them in second-hand shops and flea markets. Second-hand ceramics are individual; searching and finding a beautiful one yourself makes for good memories and means you will cherish it even more.

Ikebana

Ikebana (meaning 'living flowers') is the ancient Japanese art of flower arranging. It was developed following the Buddhist principle of minimalism, so you shouldn't use any element in your arrangement unless it has a reason to be there. Minimalism, graceful shapes and a three-pointed structure are the basic principles that are shared between the various schools of ikebana. The following tips will help you to get started.

One of the most distinctive features of ikebana is its use of a shallow vessel, although cylindrical vases are also used. The vessel relies on what's called a kenzan, a device fitted with pins that pierce through the base of stems to hold everything in the desired position. Place this at the bottom of the container, centred or off-centred depending on what you prefer, and fill the container with water until it just covers the top of the spikes. In general, you want to insert everything at some sort of angle since that's how things appear in nature. The three-pointed nature of ikebana is used to represent humanity (jin), the earth (chi) and heaven (ten). Most ikebana designs include five to thirteen stems. Space is an important part of the design, so leave some round each stem.

Materials you can use for your design include living branches, leaves, stones, moss, grasses and blossoms. It's important to remember that ikebana acknowledges the seasons. A lot of ikebana arrangements feature a bud to represent the promise of hope. Whereas Western-style arrangements go for maximum impact, ikebana flowers do not have to be in bloom at the same time. Because of its simplicity, the best place to put an ikebana arrangement is a space that is not cluttered.

Open shelves – a place to display

In Japan rooms tend to be furnished and decorated in a highly functional way, owing to a shortage of living space. One particular way of using practical items as decoration is adopted by the Japandi aesthetic. Open shelves are often decorated with just a few books, grouped glassware and beloved handmade ceramic objects. The creation of lovingly decorated shelves or corners is one of the many attractive (and fun) aspects of the Japandi aesthetic. On pages 108-127 you'll find much more about the art of decoration.

Right page: Built-in shelves called chigai-dana by Japanese architects are built into a wall. The words 'chigai' (different) and 'dana' (shelf) suggest how the shelves are hung: two or more are always arranged in a staggered layout, usually with a continuous shelf above.

Creating still lifes

There are a few tips and tricks to help you create a perfect, balanced still life with everyday objects. You can use these to construct simple yet beautiful vignettes round your home. Just choose a few objects that you find visually pleasing. Look for a variety of shapes, forms, colours and textures and form connections (by matching colours or textures) that lead the eye round the composition.

Different heights create interest. Use an odd number of, and not too many, items. Create horizontal lines (for instance with books) and also vertical ones (use tall vases). Take things out; add others in.

Use the rules of composition: the rule of thirds, the golden triangle and the golden spiral. Following these makes your still life much more interesting. Divide the image you're creating into three horizontal sections and three vertical sections in your mind. Where the lines intersect is an ideal location for the important parts of the display.

CHAPTER 3.
LET'S GET INSPIRED

Now that we have learned how Japandi manages to intertwine aspects of the Nordic concept of hygge and the ancient concept of wabi-sabi, it's time to get inspired. Let's take a tour round different types of room and see how Japandi takes them to another level of luxury and elegance. Discover how you can incorporate Japandi in your house and how to achieve that embracing, calm interior.

In a day and age where houses appear to be entirely redecorated in the span of one television show and social media make 'having style' seem like a piece of cake, it can be intimidating to decide where to begin. The reality for most of us is that we have to start with what we have and let things evolve from there. Being in a rush to finish decorating your home often means you buy things that aren't necessarily the best choice in the long run. Don't spend money on something temporary that you don't like at all. Overall, create a home that is filled with quality items and look for items you know you'll love for years to come. Let your style develop. Lastly, instead of an immediate total interior overhaul, you can start with a simple tidy-up or declutter (see page 46) to help set you on your way to creating your minimalist paradise. Japandi is about living in harmony with your environment, not about consumerism. Creating a home is like a never-ending love story.

Beauty is the harmony of purpose and form.
— Alvar Aalto (1898–1976)

Living room

There's no one size that fits a living-room area. Before you start decorating the space, you need to determine the way you want to live in it or use it. How many people will be using it? Is your living room a space for reading and conversing only or will there also be a television? Does it need to contain a small workspace or a play area for kids? Just because Japandi is uncluttered and serene doesn't mean it can't be family friendly. In short, be realistic and honest about your intentions with the space and make sure the room provides this. Make a moodboard (see page 107) to help hone your ideas about furniture, lighting and accessories. It's your home and safe haven, not a showroom!

When it comes to living-room furniture, ideal Japandi furnishings combine practical function with a sleek style. Decorations are carefully chosen and adapted for a less-is-more impact. The Danish concept of hygge is easy to incorporate with soft textiles and lots of layered textures. To keep the look Japandi, balance those soft, textured fabrics with clean-lined details such as, for example, a pair of sculptural coffee tables.

The Japanese idea of danshari (decluttering) is a concept that Japandi really celebrates. It means keeping only items that serve a purpose or have some sort of meaning for you. When furnishing your home in the Japandi aesthetic, think quality over quantity. Consider each piece carefully and you'll create your own, super-personal, tailored Japandi look.

> Remember that there's no right or wrong. Each Japandi home is different and you, as its inhabitant, know each space best. Do what works for you and what works for the space. Consider light, purpose and the needs of the people who most often use the space. Make your design personal and keep in mind that it should be embracing to all its inhabitants.

Frederik Alexander Werner (Designer & Partner at Norm Architects): 'Natural daylight always plays an important role in our projects, and in my own home. Being a renovation project, it was important to find balance between keeping some of the original atmosphere from the house, while also opening it up to bring in more natural light and connect both the interior and exterior in a more harmonious way.'

Kitchen

Open-plan kitchens are one of the most sought-after features of the modern home. They allow a room to flow, thanks to the fact that there are no visual barriers. The great appeal of the open-plan kitchen is that you can be cooking while interacting with family members or party guests.

However, no one wants to be looking at dirty dishes and other kinds of kitchen clutter, and although we all want to be on top of clearing up in real life this isn't always possible. You want to avoid a cluttered and messy kitchen space, but you don't want an empty white box either. The Japandi kitchen is functional yet stylish, warm and uncluttered, and is therefore the perfect aesthetic for an open-plan kitchen.

Japandi combines everything you need and uses an ample amount of decoration. When decorating a Japandi kitchen, consider the principles of wabi-sabi (see page 12). Choose things that have a functional purpose and that are visually pleasing. Keep small details – such as an assortment of white bowls or your morning coffee essentials – in sight to add a touch of playfulness to the minimalism. Think about items that bring joy or calm when you see them from day to day. Visually less pleasing but handy kitchen utensils or machines can be kept out of sight in a closed kitchen cabinet.

The Japandi kitchen is all about contrast: light and dark, modern and traditional, wood and stone. This adds visual interest without cluttering the space. Texture and contrast are important in a Japandi-style kitchen, so don't be afraid to add beautiful textures and earthy tones through walls, worktops or wares. Considering how a kitchen is used, it is best to use materials that are easy to maintain and clean. Read more about colour and texture on pages 70–81 and pages 93–101. And you could of course add some plants for a splash of green.

One of the most common requests from customers today is a social kitchen where you can hang out with family and friends while cooking.
— Nordiska Kök

Japandi kitchens have ample storage space and are well organized. The combination of different shades of wood, chrome and natural stone gives this kitchen a luxurious look. It also creates contrast and interest. Parts of the wall cabinets are left open to display a selection of treasured items.

The kitchen should be a space you enjoy being in, and thoughtful kitchen design can help make that happen. When designing a kitchen layout, think about what tasks you perform most frequently and ask yourself what persistent problems you experience with your current kitchen. Don't assume you have to stick to the same layout and configuration of units – you need not be afraid to reposition pipes and wires. In kitchen design, it is really important to match design to function.

CHAPTER 3. LET'S GET INSPIRED

These slatted sliding doors temporarily hide the cooking space from the adjoining space, which adds to a tranquil, decluttered feel.

Natural stone comes in a variety of finishes, each offering its own advantages. Before choosing, consider essential factors such as look, durability and resistance. Pictured: limestone, marble, terrazzo and granit.

Matching the colour of kitchen cabinets to the wall gives the space a cohesive aesthetic.

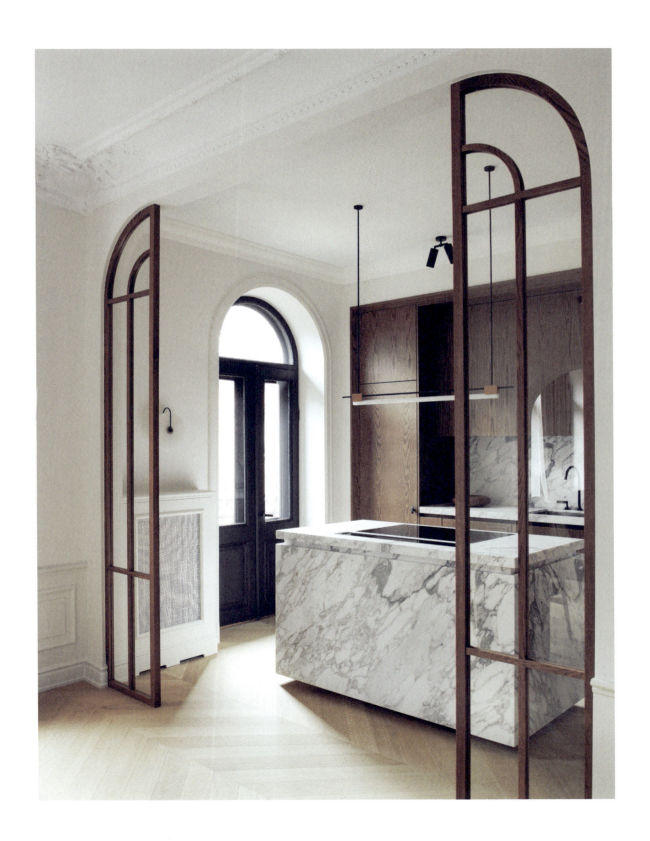

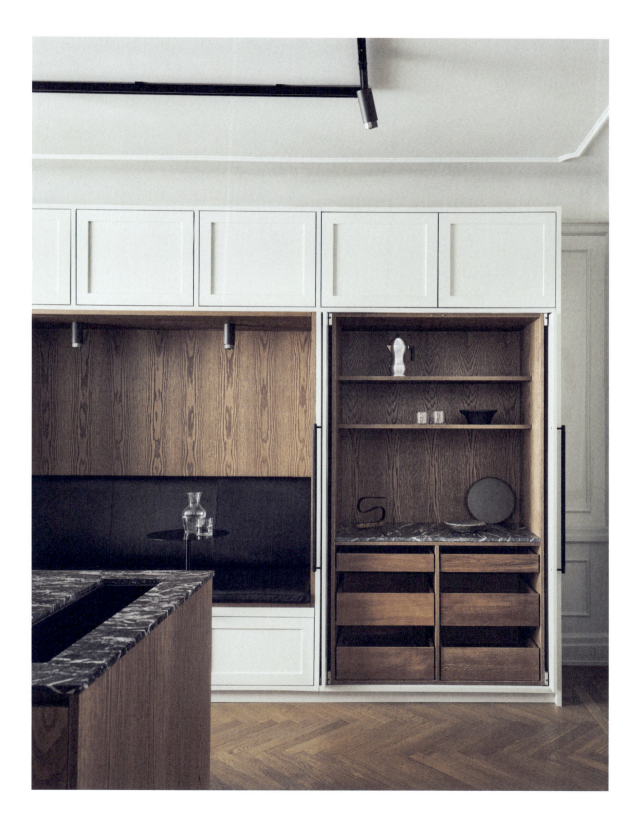

Bedroom

The styling of the bedroom is often overlooked – which perhaps isn't that strange, since you spend most of your time in there with your eyes closed. However, in a pleasantly decorated environment, you can increase feelings of wellbeing that should improve your quantity and quality of sleep.

The Japandi bedroom strikes a balance between being tranquil and luxurious. It's an inviting, calm haven where you can unwind and relax.

Japandi's attention to detail lifts the atmosphere of the bedroom. Pick out matching bedroom lamps to place at each side of the bed, and consider a dimmer switch to give your eyes and mind time to ease into the night or day. Remember that bedrooms should not be cluttered or crowded. See page 46 for tidying tips. Use very little furniture and maybe have just one well-designed chair as an extra focus. Choose a rug to add an extra cosy feeling to the room. A beautifully dressed window will help to frame the view. It also adds colour, pattern, texture and softness to the space. Bedsheets and bedcoverings, which are another focal point in the room, inject a strong element of colour and atmosphere to this space. Japandi relies entirely on natural materials, and nothing adds more to a feeling of comfort than beautiful linens made of cotton, bamboo, silk or linen. And there are benefits to using natural materials. They are, in fact, healthier for you.

Natural materials are breathable and often hypoallergenic, which means they reduce the risk of allergic reaction. Fewer toxins are used in their production than for making synthetics. Less processing means less waste, less electricity and less chemical runoff. And when natural materials finally show signs of wear, they do so with style and still look more attractive than artificial materials.

And finally, let the bedroom be a real sanctuary by keeping out phones, laptops and television sets.

Same room, different bedding, big effect. Investing in a new set of sheets, a duvet or floor cushions is an easy and relatively cheap way to change the atmosphere of a bedroom.

Frederik Alexander Werner (Designer & Partner at Norm Architects): 'Nature is an ever-present element in what we do – it's how we derive the colour schemes and create projects that not only look good but also feel good. We strive to use the inherent colours in the materials we use and by doing that we also ensure that they patinate with grace.'

Bathroom

As Japan is a country of volcanic activity, it comes as no surprise that it's home to over 25 thousand hot springs. And the Japanese love to bathe! Japanese bathing culture is focused on 'onsen' and 'sento'. An onsen is a hot spring bath that uses mineral-rich water from deep below the Earth. A sento is a public bath-house that uses standard water. Each neighbourhood has a public bathhouse and traditionally families visit them on a regular basis. The sento has a long history in the community as a place of interaction and bonding.

Scandinavia has a similar culture in which the sauna (a heated room or building) provides people with a way to relax and sweat, in addition to promoting various health benefits. The word 'sauna' comes from the Finnish word for bath or bathhouse. Saunas are intrinsic to the deep traditions in this part of the world.

The Japandi aesthetic oozes tranquillity, which makes it perfect for creating a spa-like bathroom feel. Start with a neutral shade and create contrast by adding a mix of light woods and black hues. Or use a dark base of black or charcoal-grey tiles and add Nordic elements with light neutral shades and pops of pastel colours. Whether you go for a dark or light base, keep the palette monochrome for that ultimate relaxing feel.

The bath or shower is the centrepiece of the bathroom and the focal point for your at-home spa experience. When it comes to choosing a shower, try to avoid enclosures and welcome walk-in showers or any frameless structure. Floating furniture will also help enhance a feeling of space. Opt for clean lines and minimal accessories to create your Zen sanctuary. Keep bits and bobs hidden away in a furniture unit and add texture with a couple of fluffy towels and a bath mat.

A simple way to give your bathroom that Japandi feel is finishing its walls with clay plaster instead of tiles. By seamlessly merging the finish of walls and ceilings, you create a singular, harmonious space.

Workspace

As flexible work and remote working has become more common, home offices are as much a part of the modern home as living rooms these days. When setting up your home workstation, it's best to find a space where your productivity isn't affected by any possible distractions. It's therefore ideal to set up a workspace in a spare room, attic or basement. If you don't have a spare room, look for a calm work corner in your kitchen or settle for the dining-room table. Whatever you do, don't work in your bedroom or living room; these areas are intended for rest and relaxation and should be kept as such.

A workspace is easily created with a desk and a chair. If you need a fast solution and don't have the time or the money to purchase a new home-office chair, look for other chairs in your home that will remain comfortable and supportive for long periods of sitting. Select a chair that's the right height and provides good back and arm support while you're working. A kitchen or dining table may work as a desk, too, but make sure its height works with the chair you're using. On the whole, make it all as ergonomic as possible. If you'll be working from home for significant stretches of time, it may be prudent to invest in office furniture.

Integrate a natural element by installing a houseplant – from another room if necessary – and above all keep work-related documents in your home office so that your work/life balance is in check.

Preferably, set up your workspace near a window. Natural daylight keeps you active throughout the day, and looking out of the window may help you to destress and brighten your mood. Keep your home office organized and decluttered; this will help you stay focused.

Thank you!

First, I'd like to thank all the fabulous contacts and influencers who contributed their beautiful images to this book. Special thanks go to the people of Norm Architects and Nordiska Kök.

Thanks to the team of Lannoo Publishers. To Carolijn Domensino for giving me the opportunity to make this book. And to Astrid Devlaminck for her support, teamwork and solution-oriented project management, particularly during challenging moments.

Thanks to Marlous Snijder. She was the first person to interview me in 2021 about my account @japandi.interior and the Japandi aesthetic. It was my first interview and I felt a bit nervous, but we had a lovely, relaxed chat. When Lannoo approached me to make this book, I immediately knew I wanted to do that with her. I'd like to thank Marlous not just for her amazing work, but also for her support along the way – for her optimism and positivity and the lovely chats (and photo shares) we had about our cats Gerrit (Marlous) and Kiyomi (Laila).

Special thanks to my mother Ariane Rietbergen, my father Leo Rietbergen and my brother Sander Rietbergen for their unconditional support, patience and belief in everything I do, especially during the first part of 2022. They all have a huge role in my journey, long before the start of my account and of this book. They are the main reason why I am where I am and do what I do. I therefore dedicate this book to them.

Thanks to Christian Szyinski, for his support to start my account @japandi.interior. For being a great listener and sparring partner during doubts, ideas and plans.

Last, I would like to thank you, my reader. Hopefully this book will inspire you to make your place as Japandi as you like and help you to find relaxation, calm and peace at home.

Hope to see you over @japandi.interior. Feel free to send me a message!

Love, Laila

Credits

Cover
Norm Architects, Kinuta Terrace, Photographer Jonas Bjerre-Poulsen

Backcover
Left: Norm Architects, Private Residence of Frederik Alexander Werner, Photographer Jonas Bjerre-Poulsen
Middle: Nordiska Kök, Photographer Andrea Papini
Right: ferm LIVING

Table of content
Page 4: ferm LIVING

Page 6 and 7: Norm Architects, Archipelago House, Photographer Jonas Bjerre-Poulsen

CHAPTER 1 — Japandi
Page 8: Photograph CaroLine Dethier, Interior architect Marie-Astrid Pelsser, Furniture Desiron Lizen

The minimalist home
Page 10: Norm Architects, Kinuta Terrace, Photographer Jonas Bjerre-Poulsen

Page 12: Woodchuck, styling by Tinta and photography by wij zijn kees

Page 13: Viktoria Askerow by @tthese_beautiful_thingss

Page 14 and 15: New Kintsugi repair, Humade

Page 16: Bolia

Page 19: Woodchuck, styling by Tinta and photography by wij zijn kees

The key characteristics of Japanese and Scandinavian interior
Page 20: KAD Guesthouse, Architect Keiji Ashizawa Design, Construction Fine Arts/Keiji Ashizawa Design, Photographer Jonas Bjerre-Poulsen

Page 21: Norm Architects, Kinuta Terrace, Photographer Jonas Bjerre-Poulsen

Page 23: iStock - ©Peilien

Page 25: Unsplash - @charlesdeluvio

Page 26 and 27: KAD Guesthouse, Architect Keiji Ashizawa Design, Construction Fine Arts/Keiji Ashizawa Design Photographer Jonas Bjerre-Poulsen

Page 28, 29, 30 and 31: HAY

Japandi design Icons
Page 32 and 33: Carl Hansen & Søn

Page 34: Viktoria Askerow by @tthese_beautiful_thingss

Page 35: Vitra, Akari light Isamu Noguchi

Page 36 and 37: MENU Space, Hashira Floor Lamp by Norm Architects

CHAPTER 2 — Let's Japandi
Page 38: Norm Architects, Kinuta Terrace, Photographer Jonas Bjerre-Poulsen

The principles of tidying
Page 40: Mamoesjka, www.mamoesjka.nl

Page 41: ferm LIVING

Page 42: Bolia

Page 44: Norm Architects, Gjøvik, Photographer Jonas Bjerre-Poulsen

Page 45: Norm Architects, The Audo, Photographer Jonas Bjerre-Poulsen

Page 47: Bolia

Lighting
Page 48 and 49: ferm LIVING

Page 50 and 51: Norm Architects, Private Residence of Frederik Alexander Werner, Photographer Jonas Bjerre-Poulsen

Page 52: Viktoria Askerow by @tthese_beautiful_thingss

Page 53: ferm LIVING

Page 54: WOUD Design

Page 55 and 56: ferm LIVING

Page 57: MENU space

Page 58 and 59: WOUD Design

Page 60: Photograph CaroLine Dethier, Interior architect Marie-Astrid Pelsser, Furniture Desiron Lizen

Page 61: Louis Poulsen

Page 62: MENU space

Page 63: Bolia

Page 64: Both images: Norm Architects, Kinuta Terrace, Photographer Jonas Bjerre-Poulsen

Page 65: Norm Architects, Reydon Grove, Photographer Jonas Bjerre-Poulsen

Page 66 and 67: Vitra

Colours and shapes
Page 68: Bolia

Page 69 and 71: MENU space

Page 73: Norm Architects, Private Residence of Frederik Alexander Werner, Photographer Jonas Bjerre-Poulsen

Page 74: MENU space

Page 76 and 77: Bolia

Page 78: Blue Dela Cruz, At Instagram @niblu.home

Page 79: Mamoesjka, www.mamoesjka.nl

Page 80: Norm Architects, KINFOLK, Photographer Jonas Bjerre-Poulsen

Page 81: Norm Architects, The Audo, Photographer Monica Steffensen

Page 83: Bolia

Page 84 and 85: WOUD Design

Page 86 and 87: ferm LIVING

Page 88
Left image: Nordic Studio, At Instagram @nordicstudio.nl
Right image: The home of Jessica de Geest, At Instagram @jessdegeest

Page 89: Norm Architects, Archipelago House, Photographer Jonas Bjerre-Poulsen

Page 90: ferm LIVING

Page 91: Norm Architects, The Audo, Photographer Jonas Bjerre-Poulsen

Page 92: Norm Architects, Archipelago House, Photographer Jonas Bjerre-Poulsen

Page 94: Photograph CaroLine Dethier, Interior architect Marie-Astrid Pelsser, Furniture Desiron Lizen

Page 95
Left image: Photograph CaroLine Dethier, Interior architect Marie-Astrid Pelsser, Furniture Desiron Lizen
Right image: Norm Architects, Sandbjerg Residence, Photographer Jonas Bjerre-Poulsen

Page 96: MENU space

Page 98: MENU space

Page 99: Norm Architects, Archipelago House, Photographer Jonas Bjerre-Poulsen

Page 100: Bolia

Page 101: SOFA COMPANY

Page 103: Photograph CaroLine Dethier, Interior architect Marie-Astrid Pelsser, Furniture Desiron Lizen

Page 104: Norm Architects, Private Residence of Frederik Alexander Werner, Photographer Jonas Bjerre-Poulsen

Page 105: Norm Architects, Gjøvik, Photographer Jonas Bjerre-Poulsen

Page 106: Bolia

Page 107: Bolia

Page 109: Norm Architects, Kinuta Terrace, Photographer Jonas Bjerre-Poulsen

Page 111: MENU space

Page 112: Private residence of Laila Rietbergen, Photographer Huib Noordzij for Indudoors

Page 114 and 115: ferm LIVING

Page 117: MENU space

Page 118: ferm LIVING

Page 120:
Top right image: Unsplash - © Anna Cicognani

Bottom left image: ferm LIVING

Page 122: Artist Simone Polk, At Instagram @simonepolk

Page 123 and 124: MENU space

Page 125: Norm Architects, Archipelago House, Photographer Jonas Bjerre-Poulsen

Page 126 and 127: Viktoria Askerow, @tthese_beautiful_thingss

CHAPTER 3 — Let's get inspired
Living room

Page 128: Norm Architects, Archipelago House, Photographer Jonas Bjerre-Poulsen

Page 130: Photograph CaroLine Dethier, Interior architect Marie-Astrid Pelsser, Furniture Desiron Lizen

Page 132: Norm Architects, Reydon Grove, Photographer Jonas Bjerre-Poulsen

Page 133: Photograph CaroLine Dethier, Interior architect Marie-Astrid Pelsser, Furniture Desiron Lizen

Page 134 and 135: MENU space

Page 136, 138 and 139: Norm Architects, Private Residence of Frederik Alexander Werner, Photographer Jonas Bjerre-Poulsen

Page 137: Private residence of Laila Rietbergen, Photographer Huib Noordzij for Indudoors

Page 140: Norm Architects, Gjøvik, Photographer Jonas Bjerre-Poulsen

Page 141: Photograph CaroLine Dethier, Interior architect Marie-Astrid Pelsser, Furniture Desiron Lizen

Page 142 and 143: Artist Simone Polk, At Instagram @simonepolk

Page 144 and 145: Nordic Studio, At Instagram @nordicstudio.nl

Page 146: ferm LIVING

Page 147: Blue Dela Cruz, At Instagram @niblu.home

Page 148 and 149: ferm LIVING

Page 150: ferm LIVING

Page 151: Norm Architects, Archipelago House, Photographer Jonas Bjerre-Poulsen

Kitchen

Page 152: Nordiska Kök, Photographer Andrea Papini

Page 154 and 155: Nordiska Kök, Photographer Andrea Papini

Page 156 and 157: Nordiska Kök, Photographer Andrea Papini

Page 158 and 159: Photograph CaroLine Dethier, Interior architect Marie-Astrid Pelsser, Furniture Desiron Lizen

Page 160
Top right image: Nordiska Kök, Photographer Osman Tahir
Under left image: Nordiska Kök, Photographer Andrea Papini
Under right image: Nordiska Kök, Photographer Andrea Papini

Page 161: Nordiska Kök, Photographer Andrea Papini

Page 162 and 163: Nordiska Kök, Photographer Andrea Papini

Page 164, 165, 166 and 167: Keiji Ashizawa Design & Norm Architects, Azabu Residence, Architects and Designers: Keiji Ashizawa, Kenji Kawami, Frederik Alexander Werner and Jonas Bjerre-Poulsen, Furniture manufacturer: Karimoku Case Study and Kojima Shouten, Photographer Jonas Bjerre-Poulsen

Page 168 and 169: Norm Architects, Project Archipelago House, Photographer Jonas Bjerre-Poulsen

Page 170, 171, 172 and 173: Nordiska Kök, Photographer Andrea Papini

Page 174 and 175: Keiji Ashizawa Design & Norm Architects, Azabu Residence, Architects and Designers: Keiji Ashizawa, Kenji Kawami, Frederik Alexander Werner and Jonas Bjerre-Poulsen, Furniture manufacturer: Karimoku Case Study and Kojima Shouten, Photographer Jonas Bjerre-Poulsen

Page 176 and 177: Norm Architects, Gjøvik, Photographer Jonas Bjerre-Poulsen

Page 178 and 179: Houtmerk, Photographer Frank Poppelaars

Page 180: Norm Architects, Sandbjerg Residence, Photographer Jonas Bjerre-Poulsen

Page 181: Nordiska Kök, Photographer Andrea Papini

Page 182 and 183: Nordiska Kök, Photographer Kristofer Johnsson

Page 184 and 185: Nordiska Kök, Photographer Andrea Papini

Page 186: Norm Architects, Private Residence of Frederik Alexander Werner, Photographer Jonas Bjerre-Poulsen

Page 187: Houtmerk, Photographer Frank Poppelaars

Bedroom

Page 189 and 190: ferm LIVING

Page 191: Norm Architects, The Audo, Photographer Monica Steffensen

Page 192 and 193: Viktoria Askerow by @tthese_beautiful_thingss

Page 194: ferm LIVING

Page 195: Blue Dela Cruz, At Instagram @niblu.home

Page 196 and 197: MENU space

Page 198: Norm Architects, Private Residence of Frederik Alexander Werner, Photographer Jonas Bjerre-Poulsen

Page 199: MENU space

Page 200 and 201 : Photograph CaroLine Dethier, Interior architect Marie-Astrid Pelsser, Furniture Desiron Lizen

Page 202: The home of Jessica de Geest, At Instagram @jessdegeest

Page 203: Blue Dela Cruz, At Instagram @niblu.home

Page 204: Norm Architects, The Audo, Photographer Jonas Bjerre-Poulsen

Page 205: Norm Architects, The Audo, Photographer Monica Steffensen

Page 206: YOURS boutique hotel Valencia, www.thisisyours.es, At Instagram @yourshotel, Owners Daphne Kniest and Wouter Kock

Page 207: Norm Architects, Sandbjerg Residence, Photographer Jonas Bjerre-Poulsen

Page 208 and 209: Keiji Ashizawa Design & Norm Architects, Azabu Residence, Architects and Designers: Keiji Ashizawa, Kenji Kawami, Frederik Alexander Werner and Jonas Bjerre-Poulsen, Furniture manufacturer: Karimoku Case Study and Kojima Shouten, Photographer Jonas Bjerre-Poulsen

Bathroom

Page 211: Norm Architects, Sandbjerg Residence, Photographer Jonas Bjerre-Poulsen

Page 212 and 213: COCOON

Page 214: Norm Architects, Sandbjerg Residence, Photographer Jonas Bjerre-Poulsen

Page 215: Norm Architects, Private Residence of Frederik Alexander Werner, Photographer Jonas Bjerre-Poulsen

216 and 217: Norm Architects, Sandbjerg Residence, Photographer Jonas Bjerre-Poulsen

Page 218 and 219: MENU space

Page 220 and 221: COCOON

Page 222 and 223: ferm LIVING

Page 224 and 225: MENU space

Page 226: Norm Architects, Gjøvik, Photographer Jonas Bjerre-Poulsen

Page 227: Houtmerk, Photographer Frank Poppelaars

Workspace

Page 228: MENU space

Page 230 and 231: Norm Architects, Gjøvik, Photographer Jonas Bjerre-Poulsen

Page 232 and 233: ferm LIVING

Page 234 and 235: MENU space

Page 236 and 237: Houtmerk, Photographer Frank Poppelaars

Page 238 and 239: Norm Architects, KINFOLK, Photographer Jonas Bjerre-Poulsen

Page 240 and 241: MENU space

Page 242, 243 and 244: Norm Architects, Kinuta Terrace, Photographer Jonas Bjerre-Poulsen

245: Photograph CaroLine Dethier, Interior architect Marie-Astrid Pelsser, Furniture Desiron Lizen

Page 246 and 247: Norm Architects, Private Residence of Frederik Alexander Werner, Photographer Jonas Bjerre-Poulsen

Page 248 and 249: Keiji Ashizawa Design & Norm Architects, Azabu Residence, Architects and Designers: Keiji Ashizawa, Kenji Kawami, Frederik Alexander Werner and Jonas Bjerre-Poulsen, Furniture manufacturer: Karimoku Case Study and Kojima Shouten, Photographer Jonas Bjerre-Poulsen

Page 250 and 251: Norm Architects, Kinuta Terrace, Photographer Jonas Bjerre-Poulsen

Thank you

Page 253: Laila Rietbergen and Kiyomi at home, At Instagram @japandi.interior, Photographer Ariane Rietbergen, Artwork from Werk aan de Muur, Marset Ginger wall light of Marset, Avant Candelabra of ferm LIVING

Idea and Concept

Laila Rietbergen

With her love for tradition, craftmanship and the traditional principles of wabi-sabi and hygge, Laila Rietbergen's enthusiasm for Japandi kicked off before it became a world-renowned trend. After a trip to Japan in 2018, her love blossomed and set her on the path of her Instagram account @japandi.interior, with which she inspires her followers daily with the Japandi aesthetic. For Laila, Japandi is more than a decorating style; it's a lifestyle that helps to create a minimalist and tranquil home environment.

Texts

Marlous Snijder

Marlous Snijder (@ohmariemag) lives and breathes interior, vintage, trends and design and loves to write about them. She works as a freelance interior editor, columnist and author, has written for several major Dutch publishers, and has published a book about thrift shopping. In Japandi Living her love of interior design and gift for composing beautiful sentences come together in an elegant synthesis.

Editing

First Edition Translations

Design

Tina Smedts – De Poedelfabriek

Sign up for our newsletter with news about new and forthcoming publications on art, interior design, food & travel, photography and fashion as well as exclusive offers and events. If you have any questions or comments about the material in this book, please do not hesitate to contact our editorial team: art@lannoo.com

Follow @japandi.interior to get your daily Japandi inspiration, and don't hesitate to send a DM message to Laila Rietbergen

©Lannoo Publishers, Belgium, 2022
D/2022/45/99 – NUR450/454
ISBN: 978 94 014 8371 1
Sixth print run
www.lannoo.com

All the rights reserved. No part of this publication may be reproduced or transmitted in any form or by any means, electronic or mechanical, including photography, recording or any other information storage and retrieval system, without prior permission in writing from the publisher.

Every effort has been made to trace copyright holders. If however you feel that you have inadvertently been overlooked, please contact the publishers.